D_ YELLOWSTONE NATIONAL PARK

WEST YELLOWSTONE TO OLD FAITHFUL

by Robert Stone

Photographs by Robert Stone
Published by:
Day Hike Books, Inc.
114 South Hauser Box 865
Red Lodge, MT 59068
Copyright 1995

Distributed by:
ICS Books, Inc.
1370 E. 86th Place
Merrillville, IN 46410
1-800-541-7323
Fax 1-800-336-8334

Hike 1
Upper Geyser Basin Boardwalks

Hiking Distance: 2 to 4 miles round trip
Hiking Time: 1 hour to all day
Elevation Gain: Level
Topo: U.S.G.S. Old Faithful,
         The Yellowstone Association Upper Geyser Map

Summary of hike: Although this is not a backcountry hike (except for the Observation Point Trail), it is magnificent and a favorite Yellowstone hike. The Upper Geyser Basin contains the largest group of geysers in the world.   They are in continuous motion (photo on back cover).   The predicted times of many of their eruptions are posted in the Visitor Center.   Viewing this large assortment of geysers (including Old Faithful), pools, and the Firehole River, make this walk a chance to see one of the earth's magical wonders.

Driving directions: This hike begins at the Old Faithful parking lot or Visitor Center inside Yellowstone National Park.

Hiking directions: From the parking lot, walk towards Old Faithful Geyser. The boardwalks and improved trails will lead you along various loops. Whichever direction you decide to take, you will feel you chose the right route. Observation Point, on the trail circling behind Old Faithful, gives a beautiful overview of all the magnificent thermal activity.

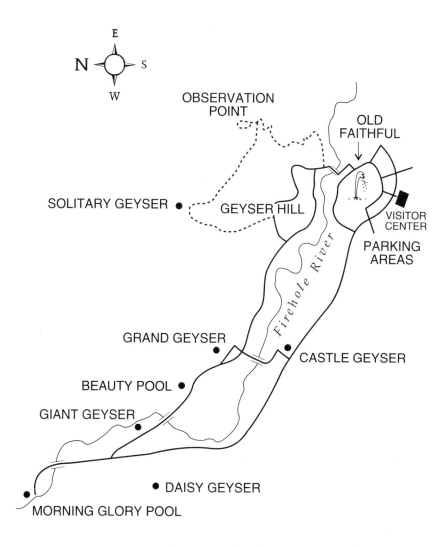

E
N ← ⊕ → S
W

OBSERVATION
POINT

OLD
FAITHFUL

SOLITARY GEYSER ●

GEYSER HILL

VISITOR
CENTER

PARKING
AREAS

Firehole River

GRAND GEYSER ●

CASTLE GEYSER ●

BEAUTY POOL ●

GIANT GEYSER ●

● DAISY GEYSER

● MORNING GLORY POOL

UPPER GEYSER BASIN
BOARDWALKS

Hike 3
Harlequin Lake Trail

Hiking Distance: 1 mile round trip
Hiking Time: 30 minutes
Elevation Gain: 120 feet
Topo: Mount Jackson

Summary of hike: The Harlequin Lake Trail is a short, easy hike to a large lake. The lake is half covered in lily pads with bright yellow flowers. A variety of birds inhabit the area. The Yellowstone fires of 1988 burned the lodge pole trees sur-rounding this trail, and now thousands of new 2' to 4' baby lodge pole trees cover the hillside.

Driving directions: Harlequin Lake is in Yellowstone National Park on the road between West Yellowstone and Madison Junction. From the West Yellowstone Park entrance, drive east 11.9 miles and turn right into the parking area on the south side of the road. From Madison Junction, drive west 1.6 miles and turn left into the parking area. On the north side of the highway is a sign marked "Harlequin Lake."

Hiking directions: Cross the highway to the Harlequin Lake trailhead. The trail gently climbs around the hill to the lake on the other side. To return, take the same trail back.

TO
WEST
YELLOWSTONE

*Harlequin
Lake*

TO
MADISON JCT

Madison River

PARKING

HARLEQUIN LAKE

Hike 4
Lone Star Geyser Trail

Hiking Distance: 5 miles round trip
Hiking Time: 2 hours
Elevation Gain: 200 feet
Topo: Old Faithful

Summary of hike: This beautiful hike runs alongside the Firehole River to a 13-foot sinter cone geyser. The Lone Star Geyser erupts in 3-hour intervals, shooting 40 feet high. It is well worth waiting for it.

Driving directions: The Lone Star Geyser Trail is in Yellowstone National Park south of Old Faithful. From Old Faithful, take the road south towards Grant Village 3.7 miles to the Lone Star Geyser parking area. It is located about 50 yards past the well-marked Kepler Cascades. Turn right and park.

Hiking directions: The trail begins at the parking area. Hike the well-defined trail all the way to Lone Star Geyser. The trail follows the Firehole River the entire distance.

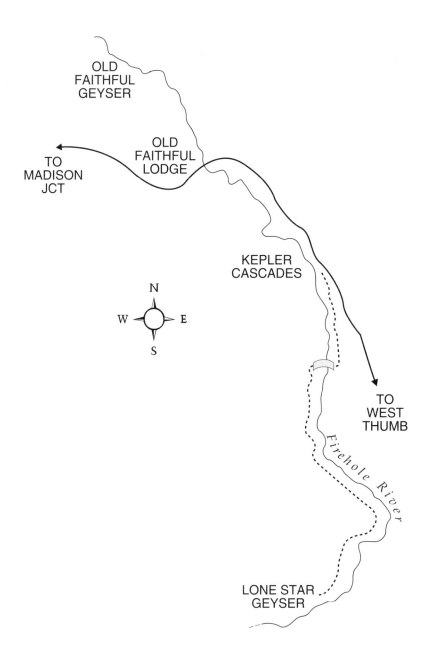

OLD
FAITHFUL
GEYSER

OLD
FAITHFUL
LODGE

TO
MADISON
JCT

KEPLER
CASCADES

N
W E
S

TO
WEST
THUMB

Firehole River

LONE STAR
GEYSER

LONE STAR GEYSER TRAIL

Grotto Geyser in the Upper Geyser Basin - Hike 1

View of Targhee Peak along Targhee Creek Trail - Hike 2

The Firehole River enroute to Lone Star Geyser – Hike 4

View of Hebgen Lake from the shadows of the lookout tower – Hike 8

Hike 5
Mystic Falls Loop

Hiking Distance: 3 miles round trip
Hiking Time: 1.5 hours
Elevation Gain: 800 feet
Topo: Old Faithful

Summary of hike: This hike follows a river to Mystic Falls, a full-bodied, powerful waterfall with a 100-foot drop. The wooden walkways at the beginning of this hike overlook thermal pools and geysers. Many people visit this area specifically to view these features.

Driving directions: Mystic Falls is in Yellowstone National Park on the road between Old Faithful and Madison Junction. From Old Faithful, drive north 2.5 miles to the Biscuit Basin parking area. Turn left and park. From Madison Junction, drive south 13.8 miles to the Biscuit Basin parking area and turn right.

Hiking directions: From the parking lot, cross the bridge over the Firehole River. Walk to the far end of the wooden boardwalk where you will find a trail that leads to Mystic Falls. At the first junction, take the lower trail to the left. This is the beginning of the loop. The lower trail takes you along the Little Firehole River to Mystic Falls. At the falls, continue on the trail as you climb to the top. From here, the trail leads through a forest back to the wooden walkways and the parking area.

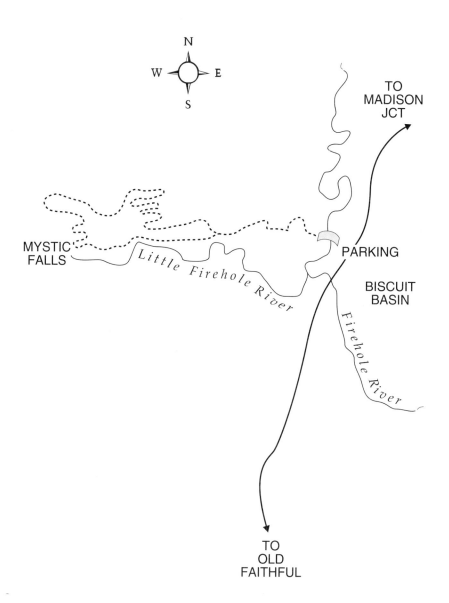

N
W E
S

TO
MADISON
JCT

MYSTIC
FALLS

Little Firehole River

PARKING

BISCUIT
BASIN

Firehole River

TO
OLD
FAITHFUL

MYSTIC FALLS LOOP

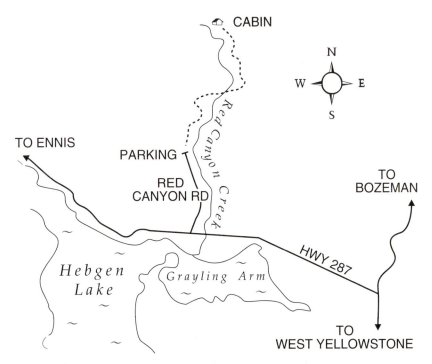

CABIN

N
W   E
S

TO ENNIS

PARKING

RED
CANYON RD

Red Canyon Creek

TO
BOZEMAN

Hebgen Lake

Grayling Arm

HWY 287

TO
WEST YELLOWSTONE

RED CANYON

Hike 6
Red Canyon

Hiking Distance: 4 miles round trip
Hiking Time: 2 hours
Elevation Gain: 600 feet
Topo: Mount Hebgen

Summary of hike: This hike follows a creek upstream through a lodgepole forest. There are beautiful rock formations, cascading waters, and several stream crossings.

Driving directions: From the town of West Yellowstone, drive north on Highway 191 (in the direction of Bozeman) for 8 miles. Turn left on Highway 287 towards Ennis. At 4.6 miles, turn right onto Red Canyon Road. This turn is marked with a Forest Service sign. Drive up Red Canyon Road 2.7 miles to the trailhead and park.

Hiking directions: Follow the trail as it leads you through the forest alongside Red Canyon Creek. Although this hike can go on for five miles to the Cabin Creek cabin, I turned around after two miles where the trail opens up to a large meadow with several knolls covered in wildflowers. To return, retrace your steps.

Hike 7
Riverside Trail

Hiking Distance: 3 miles round trip
Hiking Time: 1.5 hours
Elevation Gain: Level hiking
Topo: West Yellowstone

Summary of hike: This hike is a river stroll. It begins in the town of West Yellowstone and leads into Yellowstone National Park along a beautiful forested trail to the Madison River. In the early morning, you may see moose along the river banks.

Driving directions: In West Yellowstone, drive to the intersection of Madison Avenue and Boundary Street. These streets cross two blocks east of downtown.

Hiking directions: Begin on the east side of Boundary Street, and walk through the opening in the fence. The fence is the west boundary of Yellowstone National Park. Continue east on the trail for one mile until it meets the Madison River. The trail meanders in both directions along the river. Hike as briefly or as long as you like. Return on the same trail back to your car.

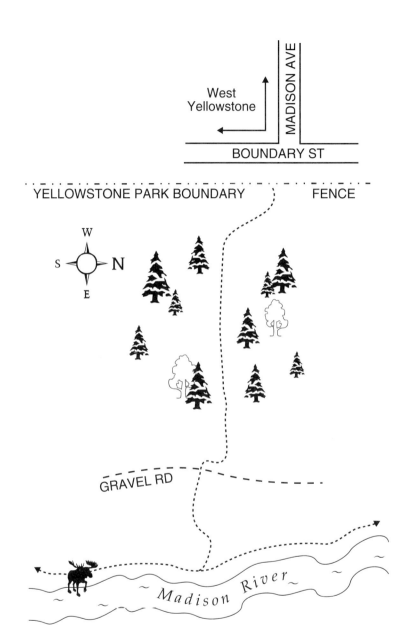

RIVERSIDE TRAIL

Hike 8
Horse Butte Lookout

Hiking Distance: 3.4 miles round trip
Hiking Time: 2 hours
Elevation Gain: 500 feet
Topo: U.S.G.S. West Yellowstone and Teepee Creek

Summary of hike: This hike overlooks Hebgen Lake, the Madison Arm, Yellowstone National Park and the Continental Divide. Along the way, the hillside meadow is covered with wildflowers. It is an excellent place to view birds, including bald eagles, osprey and pelicans.

Driving directions: From downtown West Yellowstone, drive 5 miles north on Highway 191 towards Bozeman. Turn left at Rainbow Point Road. Turn left again 3.2 miles ahead at a 4-way junction. Continue 1.6 miles to Horse Butte Lookout Road. The road, which is marked, forks to the right. This lightly used vehicle road is the hiking trail. Park anywhere along the side of the road.

Hiking directions: Hike up the road to the fire lookout tower. The road climbs 500 feet in 1.7 miles to the top. Picnic tables are available at the top. It is a great place to have lunch and look over the entire area. Return along the same route.

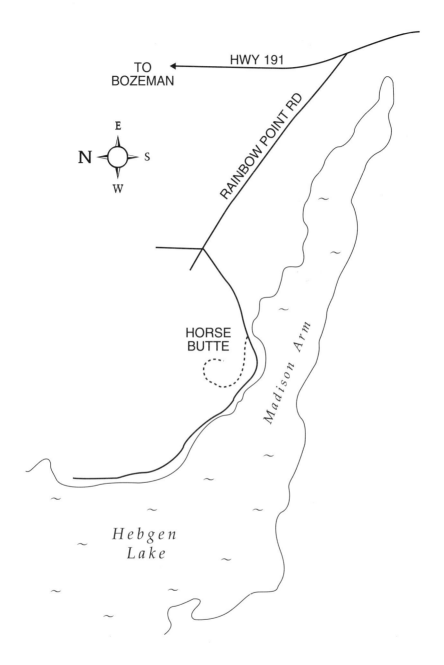

HORSE BUTTE LOOKOUT

Hike 9
Fairy Falls Trail

Hiking Distance: 4.5 miles round trip
Hiking Time: 2 hours
Elevation Gain: Level hiking
Topo: Lower Geyser Basin

Summary of hike: This near-level hike is no longer the most scenic hike in the book. The path is through a lodge pole forest that was burned to a crisp in the 1988 fire. The hike is still worth the effort. Fairy Falls has a 200-foot waterfall with a beautiful pool at its base.

Driving directions: Fairy Falls is in Yellowstone National Park on Fountain Flat Drive between Madison Junction and Old Faithful. From Madison Junction, drive south 5.6 miles and turn right on Fountain Flat Drive. From Old Faithful, drive north 10.5 miles and turn left on Fountain Flat Drive. This road ends in 2.5 miles at the parking area and trailhead, just past Goose Lake.

Hiking directions: From the parking area at the end of the road, continue walking in the same direction past the barricade. Follow the road 0.6 miles. At that point a trail sign will direct you to the right. Fairy Falls is another 1.6 miles. To return, retrace your steps.

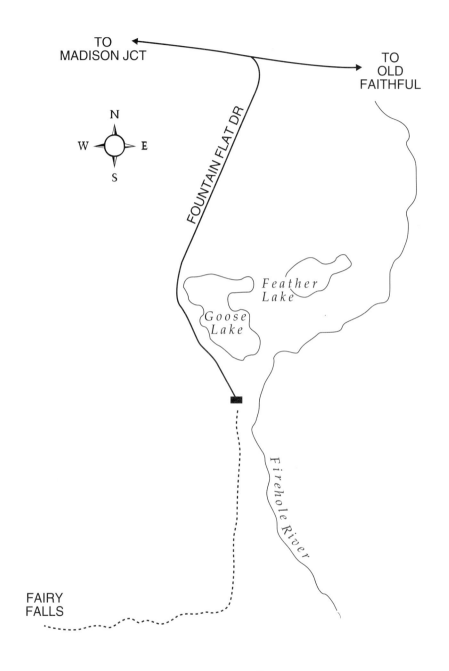

FAIRY FALLS TRAIL

NOTES

TOM EGENES

About the Author

The lure of the beautiful Rocky Mountains drew Robert to Red Lodge, Montana, in 1979. Hiking, horsepacking, and living in the Rockies has fulfilled a lifelong dream.

Robert Stone has traveled and photographed extensively throughout Asia, Europe, the Caribbean, Hawaii, and the Continental United States.

Information Sources

West Yellowstone
Chamber of Commerce
100 Yellowstone Ave.
West Yellowstone, MT
(406) 646-7701

Yellowstone National Park
(Information)
(307) 344-7381

Yellowstone Institute
P.O. Box 117
Yellowstone National Park
Wyoming 82190
(307) 344-7381 Ext. 2384

Old Faithful Visitor Center
(by Old Faithful)
(307) 344-7381 Ext. 6001

Other Day Hike Guidebooks

These books may be purchased at your local bookstore or they will be glad to order them. For a full list of titles available directly from ICS Books, call toll-free 1-800-541-7323. Visa or Mastercard accepted.

Please include $2.00 per order to cover postage and handling. Please send the books marked above. I enclose $ _____

Name _____

Address _____

City _____ State _____ Zip _____

Credit Card # _____ Exp. _____

Signature _____

Distributed by:
ICS Books, Inc.
1370 E. 86th Place, Merrillville, IN 46410
1-800-541-7323 · Fax 1-800-336-8334